Southern Dishes for the SOUL

DALE "MRS. DEE" PAYNE
COOKING WITH DEE

Southern Dishes For The Soul
Copyright ©2025 by Dale Payne

All rights reserved. No part of this book may be reproduced, copied, stored, or transmitted in any form or by any means – graphic, electronic, or mechanical, including photocopying, recording, or information storage and retrieval systems without the prior written permission of Dale Payne or HOV Publishing, except where permitted by law.

HOV Publishing is a division of HOV, LLC.
email: hopeofvision@gmail.com
www.hovpub.com

Cover & Interior Design: HOV Design Solutions
Editor: HOV Publishing Editorial Team

ISBN Hardcase: 978-1-955107-04-4

Printed in the United States of America

DEDICATION

This book is dedicated to my grandchildren: Travis, Emori, and Rylee, and to my bonus grandchildren: Passionaé and Danaja.

Some of these recipes were passed down from my mother and grandmother, and I want to prepare them so they can be enjoyed by their families.

I also want them to live limitless, knowing that there is no impossibility with God.

This book is also dedicated to my husband, who always encouraged me and enjoyed my cooking, even when the dish didn't turn out quite like I wanted it to.

TABLE OF CONTENTS

INTRODUCTION

APPETIZERS

1. Salmon Bites
2. Italian Skillet Dip
3. Honey Mustard Sauce (Fried Chicken Strips)

SOUPS & SALADS

1. Cream Mushroom Soup
2. Turnip Green Sausage Soup
3. Mama's Potato Salad
4. Broccoli Salad
5. English Pea Salad
6. Hoppin John
9. Tortilla Salad
10. Spinach Salad with Raspberry Vinaigrette Dressing

SIDE DISHES

1. Homemade Spaghetti Sauce
2. Dee's Baked Macaroni and Cheese
3. Candied Yams
4. Southern Collard Greens
5. Fried Cabbage

TABLE OF CONTENTS

BAKED GOODS
1. How to Blind Baked a Pie
2. Spinach and Sausage Quiche
3. Honey Butter Cornbread
4. Cornbread for Dressing
5. Sausage Gravy and Biscuits
6. Yeast Rolls
7. Breakfast Casserole
8. Onion and Potato Casserole

MEATS
1. Oxtails
2. Southern Fried Chicken
3. Beef Tips and Rice
4. Crab Cakes
5. Mustard Fried Catfish

SAUCES & DRESSINGS
1. Balsamic Raspberry Vinaigrette Dressing
2. Honey Mustard Sauce
3. Tartur Sauce

TABLE OF CONTENTS

DESSERTS
1. Old Fashion Pound Cake
2. Lemon Pound Cake
3. Five Flavor Pound Cake
4. Egg Pie
5. Mama Dee's Southern Sweet Potato Pie
6. Dee-licious Pecan Pie
7. Tea Cakes
8. Oatmeal Raisin Cookies
9. Peanut Butter Chocolate Chip Cookies

INTRODUCTION

Southern Dishes for the Soul by Dale "Mrs. Dee" Payne is a collection of southern dishes she grew up eating. Some of the recipes were passed down from her mother and grandmother, and some she has added her own spin; either way, they are easy, soulful, and delicious.

Growing up in Alabama in the 1950s and 60s, Dale was the oldest of six siblings. She was in the kitchen often and at an early age. Her mother and grandmother were great cooks and poured their knowledge into her. She was standing on a stool at the stove before she was tall enough to reach it from the floor.

Her father and grandfather hunted, fished, and always kept a garden. Mrs. Dee has witnessed pigs, goats, and deer being slaughtered and prepared for the dinner table. She can skin a catfish and make a beautiful, fluffy biscuit.

INTRODUCTION CONT.

Although she was a city girl, with a father, grandfather, and grandmother raised in the country, she was exposed to a lot of traditional southern ways. Making jelly and preserves was a common practice in preparation for the winter. The bounty wouldn't be complete without a good supply of okra, corn, and tomatoes for soups and stews. She fondly remembers purple fingers from shelling peas on the porch.

Mrs. Dee is deeply rooted in her faith and love for Christ. **Southern Dishes for the Soul** is more than a collection of delicious recipes. As you browse these pages, your spirit will be fed with scripture and common-sense wisdom to uplift and inspire you.

If you need a delicious meal to prepare or an encouraging word, both can be found on these pages.

Southern Dishes
APPETIZERS

Ingredients
Dipping Sauce

- 1 cup mayonnaise
- 1 tbsp ketchup
- 1 tsp hot sauce
- 1 tsp lemon juice

Instructions:
Combine all ingredients and stir until well blended. Chill for 10 minutes before serving.

SALMON BITES with Sauce

Ingredients

- 1 filet of salmon
- 1 cup cornmeal
- ½ cup flour
- Mustard (for coating)
- Oil for frying
- 1 tsp black pepper
- Salt to taste
- 1 tbsp Old Bay seasoning

SALMON BITES

Instructions

- Wash the salmon, remove the skin, and pat dry.
- Coat the salmon with mustard and season with salt, pepper, and Old Bay seasoning.
- Cut the salmon into bite-sized pieces.
- Pour oil into a large skillet (approx. 2-3 inches deep) and heat over medium-high heat to 365°F.
- In a separate bowl, combine cornmeal and flour. Optionally, season the mix with the same seasoning used on the fish.
- Toss the salmon pieces in the cornmeal mixture until well coated.
- Carefully place coated salmon into the hot oil.
- Fry for 5-7 minutes or until golden brown and fully cooked.
- Remove and drain on a paper towel.

INSPIRATIONAL NOTE:

"God will meet all needs according to His glorious riches in Christ Jesus." — Philippians 4:19

ITALIAN SKILLET DIP

Ingredients

- ½ lb ground beef
- ½ lb ground Italian sausage
- ½ onion, chopped
- ½ bell pepper, chopped
- 4 oz cream cheese (soft)
- 1 cup sharp cheddar cheese, shredded
- 4-5 slices of frozen garlic bread
- 1 tsp each: garlic powder and onion powder
- 1 tbsp oregano and basil
- 3 cloves fresh garlic, minced
- 15 oz jar of spaghetti sauce

ITALIAN SKILLETT DIP

Instructions

- Preheat oven to 400°F.
- In a large cast iron skillet, brown ground beef and Italian sausage. Drain off grease once meat is completely browned.
- Add onions and peppers, cooking until tender.
- Add seasoning and minced garlic. Stir in cream cheese and half of the shredded cheese. Stir until cheese is melted.
- Add spaghetti sauce and stir until well combined.
- Cut garlic bread into 4 pieces and place around the skillet.
- Spread remaining cheese on top.
- Place skillet in oven and cook until bread is brown and toasted, and dip is bubbling.
- Use bread for dipping. Enjoy!

INSPIRATIONAL NOTE:

Those who bring sunshine to others cannot keep it from themselves.

Ingredients
Dipping Sauce

- ½ cup yellow mustard
- 2 tbsp mayonnaise
- 3 tbsp honey
- 1 tsp dry mustard
- ½ tsp lemon juice

HONEY MUSTARD SAUCE

Instructions

- Mix all ingredients together in a bowl.
- Stir until well combined.
- For best results, chill for a couple of hours in the refrigerator before serving.
- Enjoy!

INSPIRATIONAL NOTE:
Love your family, work super hard, and live your passion.

CREAM MUSHROOM SOUP

Ingredients

- 10 oz mushrooms
- 3 cups chicken broth
- 1 tsp salt
- 1 tsp pepper
- 3 tsp flour
- 3 tbsp butter
- 1 tsp oil (olive or vegetable)
- 1 tsp each onion powder and garlic powder
- 1 cup heavy whipping cream

Enjoy!!!

Serve warm and enjoy as a soup, or use it as a base in recipes like mushroom chicken or any dish that calls for cream of mushroom soup.

e moment you decid
etter at your chosen
me, you'll become m
rore to learn. My jo

CREAM MUSHROOM SOUP

Instructions

- Clean mushrooms with a damp paper towel. Wipe down the outside, remove the stems, and clean under the cap. Cut mushrooms into pieces or slices.
- In a medium saucepan, heat butter and oil over medium heat.
- Add mushrooms and cook for about 5 minutes until tender.
- Stir in flour and cook for 1 minute to allow the flour to blend.
- Add chicken broth, salt, pepper, onion powder, and garlic powder. Stir well.
- Continue cooking for 1-2 minutes, stirring, until the mixture begins to thicken.
- Add heavy whipping cream and stir to combine. Cook for an additional 5 minutes.

FAITH-FILLED FLAVOR:

"Agree with Him in all your ways, and He will make your path straight." - Proverbs 3:6

TURNIP GREEN SAUSAGE SOUP

Ingredients

- 1 small bunch of turnip greens
- 1 onion, diced
- 1 (16 oz) can of Great Northern beans, rinsed and drained
- 1 (16.5 oz) smoked sausage, diced
- 2 mini sweet peppers or red bell pepper, diced
- 1 tbsp sugar
- 1 tbsp apple cider vinegar
- ½ tsp red pepper flakes (optional)
- Smoked turkey (optional)
- Salt and pepper to taste

TURNIP GREEN SAUSAGE SOUP

Instructions

- Wash the greens thoroughly and roughly chop, removing the stems.
- If using smoked turkey, place the meat (e.g., turkey necks) in a large pot, cover with water, and boil until the meat is tender and pulls easily off the bone. Remove the meat and return it to the pot with the broth.
- Add turnip greens to the broth.
- Add diced onions and peppers.
- Rinse and drain the beans, then add them to the pot along with sugar, vinegar, red pepper flakes, salt, and pepper.
- In a skillet, brown the sausage.
- Once browned, add the sausage to the pot.
- Continue to cook the soup on medium heat for 20-25 minutes.
- Tip: Serve hot with cornbread

SCRIPTURE INSPIRATION:

"Happy are the people whose God is the Lord."
- Psalm 144:15

Ingredients

- 3-4 lbs Yukon Gold potatoes
- 4 eggs
- 3 tbsp sugar
- 1 cup mayonnaise
- 2 tbsp yellow mustard
- ¼ cup sweet pickle relish
- ¼ cup chopped onions
- ¼ cup chopped bell pepper
- 1 rib celery, chopped
- 1 tsp onion and garlic powder
- 1 tbsp apple cider vinegar
- ½ tsp salt and black pepper

MAMA'S POTATO SALAD

Tip

A perfect side dish for any lunch or dinner!

MAMA'S POTATO SALAD

Instructions

- Wash potatoes and place in a large pot. Cover with cold water and boil over high heat until fully cooked (a fork should easily pierce the potatoes and the skins should peel off easily).
- Boil eggs in a small pot. Cover with cold water and bring to a boil over high heat. Boil for 10 minutes, then remove and cool in cold water. Once cooled, peel and dice the eggs.
- Once potatoes are cooked, peel and chop to your desired size. (I like mine creamy and a little chunky.)
- In a large bowl, mix the potatoes with chopped eggs, mayonnaise, mustard, relish, onions, bell pepper, celery, sugar, vinegar, and seasonings. Stir well to combine.
- Cover and refrigerate for a couple of hours before serving to allow it to chill.

FAITH-FILLED FLAVOR:

"God's faithfulness and righteousness is unwavering and can be trusted."

BROCCOLI SALAD

Ingredients

- 2 heads of broccoli florets, cut into bite-sized pieces
- ½ cup diced red onions
- ½ cup raisins
- ¼ cup pecans
- 3 strips of bacon
- ½ cup shredded carrots

Dressing Ingredients

- 1 cup mayonnaise
- 3 tbsp apple cider vinegar
- 2 tbsp granulated sugar
- Salt and pepper to taste
- 1 tsp onion powder

BROCCOLI SALAD

Instructions

- Cook the bacon until crisp. Once cooled, chop into small pieces and set aside.
- In a small bowl, whisk together all dressing ingredients until smooth.
- In a large mixing bowl, combine broccoli florets, onions, raisins, pecans, and shredded carrots.
- Pour the dressing over the salad ingredients and mix well until evenly coated.
- Sprinkle chopped bacon on top.
- Refrigerate for at least 1 hour before serving.

Tip

This dish is a colorful and crunchy side that pairs well with grilled meats or as a fresh addition to any potluck or picnic spread!

ENGLISH PEA SALAD

Ingredients

- 2 (16 oz) cans English peas, drained
- 3 hard-boiled eggs, chopped
- 3 strips crispy bacon, crumbled
- 1 stalk celery, finely chopped
- ⅓ red onion, finely chopped
- ⅓ red bell pepper, finely chopped
- ¼ cup mayonnaise
- ¼ cup shredded sharp cheese
- ¼ cup sweet pickle relish
- 1 tbsp onion powder
- 1 tbsp garlic powder
- 1 tbsp sugar
- 1 tsp black pepper

ENGLISH PEA SALAD

Instructions

- In a large bowl, combine all ingredients except the mayonnaise.
- Add mayonnaise gradually, stirring after each addition until the salad is well mixed and creamy.
- Top with crumbled bacon.

Enjoy!!!

FAITH-FILLED FLAVOR:

"The little that a righteous man has is better than the riches of the wicked." - Psalm 37:16

Ingredients

- 1 lb dried black-eyed peas
- 1 ham hock or smoked jowl
- 1 onion, diced
- 1 bell pepper, diced
- ½ lb smoked sausage
- 2 cups white rice
- 3 cups chicken broth
- 1 stalk celery, diced
- Salt and pepper to taste

HOPPIN' JOHN

Tip _____

Either way, it's Dee-licious! Enjoy!

HOPPIN' JOHN

Instructions

- In a large pot, place the black-eyed peas, ham hock (or smoked jowl), salt, pepper, celery, bell pepper, onion, and chicken broth.
- Bring to a boil, then reduce heat to medium-low and cook for 2 hours.
- While peas are cooking, slice sausage into 1-inch pieces and brown in a skillet.
- Remove the ham hock, cut into bite-sized pieces, and return to the pot with the browned sausage.
- You can either:
- Add rice directly to the pot and cook for 20-25 minutes until tender (adding more broth or water if needed), or
- Cook the rice separately and serve with the pea mixture on top.

INSPIRATIONAL NOTE:

"Do your best to add holy living to your faith. Then add to this better understanding." - 2 Peter 1:5

Ingredients

- 1 (16 oz) can diced tomatoes
- 1 onion, chopped
- 3 cloves garlic
- 3 jalapeño peppers, diced
- 1 lb ground meat (beef or turkey)
- 1 bell pepper
- 1 tsp garlic, onion, and chili powder
- ½ tsp red pepper flakes, salt, and pepper
- 1 cup whole kernel corn
- 3 cups chicken broth

TORTILLA SOUP

Enjoy!!!

TORTILLA SOUP

Instructions

- In a large pot, brown the meat and drain. Return to pot and add onions, peppers, garlic, and tomatoes. Stir in spices and add chicken broth. Let mixture warm over medium heat for about 10 minutes.
- Add corn and cook over medium heat 10 more minutes.
- Serve hot topped with cheese, avocado, tortilla chips, and a squeeze of lime.

INSPIRATIONAL NOTE:

God has not given us a spirit of fear or timidity, but of power, love, and self-discipline.
— 2 Timothy 1:7

SPINACH SALAD WITH RASPBERRY VINAIGRETTE DRESSING

Ingredients

- 4 strips of bacon, cooked and chopped
- 1 (16 oz) bag of fresh raw spinach
- ¼ purple onion, thinly sliced
- 1 cup fresh strawberries, sliced
- ½ cup chopped pecans
- ½ cup feta cheese (optional)
- Raspberry vinaigrette dressing

Instructions

- Wash spinach and dry thoroughly using a clean kitchen towel. Pat dry with a paper towel to remove all excess moisture.
- In a large bowl, add spinach, sliced onions, strawberries, and chopped pecans.
- Drizzle raspberry vinaigrette dressing over the salad and toss gently to coat the spinach.
- Sprinkle chopped bacon and optional feta cheese on top.

Enjoy this vibrant and refreshing salad. The perfect side dish!

HOMEMADE SPAGHETTI SAUCE

Ingredients

- 1 lb ground beef
- 1 medium onion, chopped
- 1 bell pepper, chopped
- 3-4 mini sweet peppers, chopped
- 1 (6 oz) can tomato paste
- 1 cup beef broth
- 2 tbsp sugar
- 1 tsp salt
- 1 tsp black pepper
- 2 tbsp Italian seasoning
- 1 tbsp minced garlic
- 1 tsp onion and garlic powder
- ½ tsp thyme
- 1 bay leaf
- ¼ tsp red pepper flakes (optional)
- 1 (14.5 oz) can diced tomatoes
- 1 (30 oz) can tomato sauce

HOMEMADE SPAGHETTI SAUCE

Instructions

- In a large deep pot, add ground beef, onions, and peppers.
- Cook over medium-high heat, chopping the meat with a spatula or ground meat chopper to break it up.
- Once the meat is browned and the vegetables are tender, drain off any excess fat.
- To the pot, add diced tomatoes, tomato paste, and tomato sauce. Stir to combine.
- Add beef broth, seasonings, and bay leaf.
- Bring the mixture to a boil, then reduce the heat and cover.
- Simmer for 30 minutes.
- While the sauce simmers, cook your pasta.

Tip _____

Serve hot and enjoy!

KITCHEN WISDOM:

Love is mandatory. Hate is a choice.

DEE'S BAKED MACARONI AND CHEESE

Ingredients

- 1 lb box elbow macaroni noodles
- 1 stick of butter
- 1 block cream cheese (softened)
- 2 cups Gouda cheese (shredded)
- 2 cups Gruyere cheese (shredded)
- 2 cups whole milk
- 2 cups half and half
- 1 tbsp yellow mustard
- 1 tsp black pepper
- ½ tsp salt

Baking

Pour mixture into the prepared baking dish. Sprinkle the remaining cheese pile on top. Cover and bake for 20-25 minutes at 350°F. Remove from oven and uncover. Return to oven and bake an additional 10-15 minutes until slightly golden brown and dish is bubbling.

DEE'S BAKED MACARONI AND CHEESE

Instructions

- Preheat oven to 350°F. Grease a 9x13 baking dish and set aside.
- Bring a large pot of salted water to a boil. Cook macaroni to al dente (about 3-4 minutes), drain, and drizzle with a little olive oil (about 1 tbsp). Toss to coat noodles; this helps prevent sticking. Set aside.
- Shred cheese and mix together. Separate into 3 even piles with ⅔ in one pile and ⅓ in the other.
- In a medium saucepan over medium heat, melt butter. Add whole milk and half and half. When milk is warm, add cream cheese, stirring constantly until melted. Add the large pile of shredded cheese and stir until melted and the mixture is smooth. Remove from heat and stir in mustard, salt, and pepper.
- Pour noodles into a pot and stir to combine.

KITCHEN NOTE:
"The days are too precious to let them slip away. Find time, make time, take time to do something worthwhile."

CANDIED YAMS

Ingredients

- 2 lbs sweet potatoes
- ½ cup brown sugar
- 1 cup white sugar
- ⅓ cup orange juice
- 2 tsp cinnamon
- 1 tsp nutmeg
- ½ tsp salt
- 2 tbsp vanilla extract
- 1 stick butter (melted)

Enjoy!!!

CANDIED YAMS

Instructions

- Scrub and peel yams. Cut into ¼-inch rounds.
- Place in a 9x13 baking dish and set aside.
- In a medium bowl, combine brown sugar, white sugar, orange juice, cinnamon, nutmeg, salt, vanilla, and melted butter. Stir mixture to combine well.
- Pour mixture over the sweet potatoes and stir to make sure the potatoes are evenly coated.
- Cover with foil and place in a preheated 350°F oven. Bake for 40 minutes.
- Remove foil and baste. Bake for an additional 20-25 minutes or until potatoes are fork tender.
- Remove from oven and enjoy!

KITCHEN NOTE:

Look on the bright side and don't let adversity keep you from winning.

SOUTHERN COLLARD GREENS

Ingredients

- 1 bunch collard greens
- 1 onion (chopped)
- 3-4 sweet mini peppers
- 2 tbsp apple cider vinegar
- Smoked meat
- 2 tsp onion powder
- 2 tsp red pepper flakes
- 1 tbsp sugar

Enjoy!!!

SOUTHERN COLLARD GREENS

Instructions

- Wash and boil meat until tender.
- Cut the onion and peppers and add to the pot along with remaining ingredients.
- Wash and cut greens by rolling up and slicing into ribbons.
- Add greens to the pot. Cook until tender; they will not be crunchy.
- Enjoy with a side of cornbread!

INSPIRATIONAL NOTE:

If we confess our sins, He is faithful and just and will forgive us. — 1 John 1:9

FRIED CABBAGE

Ingredients

- 5 strips bacon
- 1 onion, chopped
- 1 bell pepper, chopped
- 1 head of cabbage
- Salt and pepper to taste

Instructions

- Cut bacon into small pieces and fry in a skillet until crispy. Remove from skillet and set aside.
- Wash and cut cabbage.
- Add onions, peppers, and cabbage to the skillet with the bacon grease.
- Season with salt and pepper to taste.
- Cook on medium-high heat for 10-15 minutes, or until vegetables are fork-tender.

QUOTE:
The things that are most valuable have nothing to do with money.

Southern Dishes
BAKED GOODS

Ingredients

- Many of the pie recipes in this book require the crust to be blind baked. This essential step helps prevent a soggy, undercooked crust, especially with wet fillings like custards, fruit, or cream pies.

HOW TO BLIND BAKE A PIE CRUST

Tip

When making pies with custard bases or moist fillings such as pumpkin, pecan, or sweet potato, blind baking is crucial. It helps ensure the bottom crust is fully cooked and not soggy.

HOW TO BLIND BAKE A PIE CRUST

Instructions

- Preheat your oven to 425°F. (If using a frozen crust, allow it to thaw completely first.)
- Line the crust with parchment paper or aluminum foil, making sure it fits snugly against the bottom and sides of the crust.
- Add pie weights, dried beans or rice can be used as a substitute. Weights should fully cover the bottom.
- Place the pie crust on a baking sheet and bake until the edges begin to turn golden brown.
- Remove from oven and carefully take out the pie weights and lining.
- If the bottom still looks wet, return the uncovered crust to the oven and bake for an additional 8-10 minutes, or until it looks dry and lightly golden.
- Follow the same steps for homemade crusts.

SPINACH AND SAUSAGE QUICHE

Ingredients

- 1 (9-inch) frozen pie crust
- 3 eggs
- 1⅓ cups fresh spinach, chopped
- ¾ lb smoked sausage
- 1 cup gouda cheese
- ½ cup heavy whipping cream
- ½ cup whole milk
- ½ tsp salt and pepper

Enjoy!!!

SPINACH AND SAUSAGE QUICHE

Instructions

- Blind bake the pie shell according to package instructions. Allow to cool.
- Preheat oven to 350°F.
- In a medium bowl, whisk together eggs, heavy cream, milk, salt, and pepper until well combined.
- Slice sausage into 1-inch rounds and brown in a skillet. Drain on a paper towel.
- Line the bottom of the cooled pie crust with half of the cooked sausage.
- Layer half of the chopped spinach and half of the gouda cheese on top.
- Repeat layers with remaining sausage, spinach, and cheese.
- Pour the egg mixture evenly over the filling.
- Place the quiche on a baking sheet and bake for 50-55 minutes, or until the top is golden and the center is set.
- Let quiche stand for at least 10 minutes before cutting.

KITCHEN NOTE:

Be a joyous spirit and a sensitive soul.

HONEY BUTTER CORNBREAD

Ingredients

- 1½ cups yellow self-rising cornmeal
- ¾ cup self-rising flour
- 2 eggs
- ¼ cup melted butter
- ¼ cup vegetable oil
- 1 cup whole milk
- 3 tablespoons honey
- ¼ cup sugar

Enjoy!!!

HONEY BUTTER CORNBREAD

Instructions

- Preheat oven to 400°F.
- Add butter and oil to a 9-10 inch cast iron skillet. Place skillet in the oven to melt butter and heat — about 1-2 minutes.
- In a large bowl, combine cornmeal, flour, sugar, eggs, and milk.
- Stir in the melted butter and oil mixture, mixing well until smooth.
- Pour batter into the preheated skillet and bake for 25-30 minutes, or until the cornbread is golden.
- Drizzle with honey immediately after removing from the oven.

INSPIRATIONAL NOTE:

Keep your spirits up. Make your heart happy.

CORNBREAD FOR DRESSING

Ingredients

- 1 cup self-rising flour
- 2 cups self-rising cornmeal
- 2 eggs
- ¼ cup melted butter
- ¾ cup vegetable oil
- 3 stalks celery
- 1 whole medium onion
- 1 whole medium bell pepper
- 2 cups whole milk

Enjoy!!!

CORNBREAD FOR DRESSING

Instructions

- Preheat oven to 425°F.
- Sauté celery, onion, and bell pepper in butter over medium-low heat until softened.
- In a large bowl, mix the remaining ingredients.
- Stir in the sautéed vegetables.
- Pour mixture into a greased 9-10 inch cast iron skillet (preferred).
- Bake for 20-25 minutes, or until golden brown and set.

INSPIRATIONAL NOTE:

Hearts united in peace can ignite truth.

Ingredients

- 1 lb ground sausage
- ¼ cup all-purpose flour
- 4 tbsp butter
- 3 cups whole milk
- ½ tsp black pepper
- ½ tsp seasoned salt

SAUSAGE GRAVY
and Biscuits

Instructions

- In a large skillet, scramble the sausage over medium heat until there is no more pink, about 8-10 minutes. Reduce heat to low.
- Add butter to skillet. Sprinkle flour over sausage, stirring approximately 2 minutes to allow the raw taste of flour to cook off.
- While stirring, add the milk and increase heat to medium-high.
- Add your seasoning and reduce heat. Let simmer for 8-10 minutes, stirring occasionally until thickened.

Ingredients

- 1 cup self-rising flour (plus more for kneading)
- ¾ cup heavy whipping cream

Tip

Delicious, topped with sausage gravy or jelly.

SAUSAGE GRAVY and Biscuits

Instructions

- Preheat oven to 500°F. Grease a 9-10 inch cast iron skillet.
- In a bowl, combine flour and heavy cream. Mix until a sticky dough is formed.
- Remove dough from bowl and place on a floured surface. Knead until dough comes together.
- Roll into a circle about ½-inch thick. Dust with flour and fold over. Knead and roll again into a circle.
- Cut out biscuits with biscuit cutter and place in greased skillet.
- Brush tops with heavy whipping cream.
- Bake in preheated oven until biscuits are golden brown, about 10-12 minutes. Enjoy!

YEAST ROLLS

Ingredients

- 1 cup hot water
- 3 tbsp white sugar
- 2 tbsp shortening
- 1 pkg active dry yeast
- 2 ¾ cups all-purpose flour
- 1 egg, beaten
- 1 tsp salt

Enjoy!!!

YEAST ROLLS

Instructions

- Mix hot water, sugar, and shortening in a large bowl. Allow to cool to lukewarm.
- Add beaten egg and package of yeast to the mixture. Let sit until mixture starts to foam.
- Mix in flour and salt until dough comes together.
- Cover dough and place in a warm area away from drafts. Let rise for approx. 30 minutes, or until doubled in size.
- Grease a muffin pan.
- Pull off enough dough to make a 2-3 inch ball, and drop two balls into each muffin cup.
- Let rise again until doubled in size (about 30 minutes).
- Place in a preheated 425°F oven and bake for 7-8 minutes or until golden brown.
- Spread soft butter on top.

INSPIRATIONAL NOTE:
"A man is rich according to what's inside of him, not by what's in his pockets."

BREAKFAST CASSEROLE

Enjoy!!!

Ingredients

- 4 eggs
- 1½ pounds sausage (ground)
- ½ cup diced onions
- ⅓ cup diced bell peppers
- 2 cups Gouda cheese or sharp cheddar
- 2 cups frozen hashbrowns, shredded and thawed
- Salt and pepper to taste
- ½ cup heavy whipping cream or whole milk
- 2 tbsp butter or oil (olive or vegetable)
- 9x9 baking dish

SCRIPTURE QUOTE:
"In him was life, and that life was the light of all mankind." - John 1:4

BREAKFAST CASSEROLE

Instructions

- Preheat oven to 350°F. Spray baking dish with cooking spray or coat dish well with butter and set aside.
- In a large skillet, melt butter and sauté peppers and onions until tender. Remove from skillet and set aside.
- Place sausage in pan and brown completely. Drain oil off and place hashbrowns in pan. Cook until lightly brown and remove from heat.
- Place sausage, peppers, and onions into the baking dish. Spread 1 cup cheese on top.
- In a mixing bowl, whisk heavy cream, eggs, salt, and pepper until well combined. Pour over top of mixture in baking dish.
- Spread remaining cheese on top.
- Place in preheated oven and cook until bubbling and slightly brown on top, approximately 30-35 minutes.
- If casserole starts to get too brown, you may cover with foil.
- Serve with buttered biscuits or toast. Enjoy!

ONION AND POTATO CASSEROLE

Ingredients

- 4 cups thinly sliced potatoes
- 1 large onion, sliced
- 3 tablespoons butter
- 3 tablespoons flour
- 1½ cups milk
- 1½ cups shredded cheese

Enjoy!!!

ONION AND POTATO CASSEROLE

Instructions

- Melt butter in a saucepan. Stir in flour slowly, then whisk in milk and season to taste.
- Cook sauce on low, stirring occasionally with a whisk until smooth. Reduce heat and add cheese.
- Continue to stir until mixture is smooth.
- Place half of the sliced potatoes in a greased 9x13 baking dish.
- Spread a layer of sliced onions over the potatoes and cover with some of the cheese sauce.
- Repeat layers until all onions and potatoes are used.
- Cover with remaining sauce and spread a layer of cheese on top.
- Cover and place in a preheated 350°F oven. Bake for 35 minutes.
- Remove cover and return to oven. Cook for an additional 10-15 minutes, or until the top is slightly browned.

SCRIPTURE INSPIRATION:
"He that walketh with wise men shall be wise: but a companion of fools shall be destroyed."
— Proverbs 13:20

NOTES

**Where the Spirit of the Lord is, there is freedom.
— 2 Corinthians 3:17**

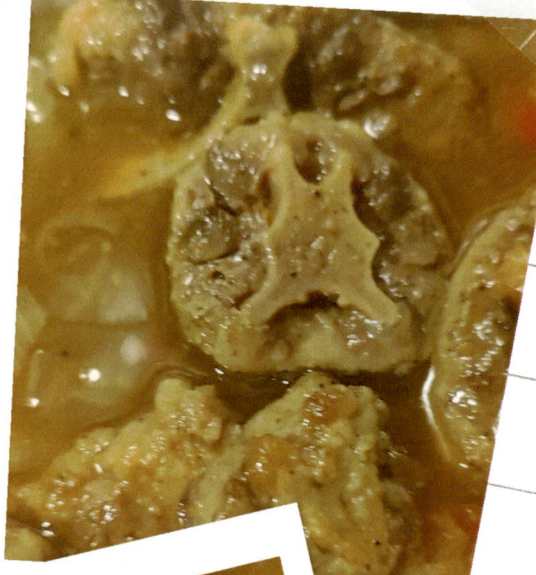

Ingredients

- 4-5 lbs oxtails
- 1 large onion
- 1 large bell pepper
- 2 cloves garlic
- ¼ cup vegetable oil (more if needed)
- 1 cup flour
- 1 tsp each: garlic powder, onion powder, thyme, salt, pepper
- 1 tsp red pepper flakes

OXTAILS

Tip

Delicious served over white or yellow rice.

OXTAILS

Instructions

- Preheat oven to 350°F.
- Wash oxtails in vinegar or lemon juice. Trim away fat and rinse.
- Let oxtails soak in salt water for 5-10 minutes.
- Rinse and pat dry.
- In a bowl, mix seasoning and flour. Drizzle oil over oxtails and coat in flour mixture.
- In a large pot, heat oil to medium-high and sear oxtails on all sides.
- Remove from pot and set aside.
- Lower heat to medium and add oil and flour to pot, stirring until mixture turns brown.
- Add meat back to pot.
- Add 3 cups of broth or water.
- Cover pot and cook in oven for 2½-3 hours or until meat reaches desired tenderness.
- Delicious served over white or yellow rice.

NOTE:
It's never too late to do ordinary things in an extraordinary way.

SOUTHERN FRIED CHICKEN

Ingredients

- 1 whole chicken, cut into parts
- 2 cups flour (self-rising)
- 1 tsp each: onion powder, garlic powder, paprika, black pepper, salt
- 3/4 cup buttermilk
- Vegetable oil for frying
- 8-10-gallon pot
- 1/2 cup corn starch

Enjoy!!!

SOUTHERN FRIED CHICKEN

Instructions

- Heat oil to 325°F in a large pot.
- Cut up whole chicken into eight pieces. Wash and pat dry.
- Pour buttermilk over chicken and season. You may use more or less than the seasonings listed. Cover and set in refrigerator for one hour.
- Combine flour, corn starch, and seasoning. Season flour and chicken.
- Toss chicken in flour, making sure chicken is well coated.
- After oil is heated, place chicken in the hot oil, skin side down. Fry until skin is golden brown (6-7 minutes).
- Turn chicken over and continue to fry until chicken is done, approximately 6-7 minutes.
- Remove from oil and drain on a rack or paper towel.
- Enjoy!

INSPIRATIONAL QUOTE:

"Feed your faith and your doubts will starve to death."

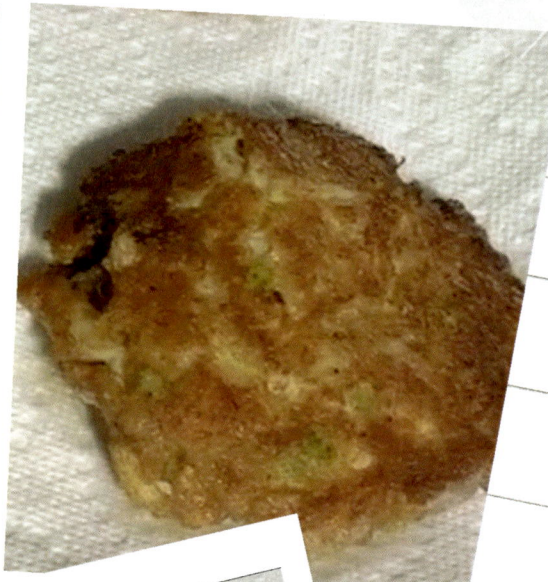

CRAB CAKES

Ingredients

- 1 lb lump crab meat
- ½ cup Ritz cracker crumbs
- ¼ cup mayonnaise
- 1 egg
- 1 tsp lemon juice
- 1 tsp yellow mustard
- 1 stalk celery, finely diced
- 1 tsp minced garlic
- 1 tsp onion powder
- ½ tsp salt
- ½ tsp black pepper
- 2 tbsp butter, melted
- 2 tbsp oil (olive or vegetable)

Tip

Serve warm with tartar sauce. Enjoy!

CRAB CAKES

Instructions

- Heat 2 tbsp oil and 2 tbsp butter in a large skillet over medium-low heat.
- In a large mixing bowl, whisk together mayonnaise, egg, lemon juice, mustard, celery, garlic, onion powder, salt, pepper, and melted butter.
- Gently fold in crab meat and cracker crumbs with a spatula, being careful not to break up the lumps.
- Form into patties and place in the skillet.
- Cook each crab cake for approximately 5 minutes per side, or until golden brown.
- Remove and drain on paper towels.

SCRIPTURE INSPIRATION:

"Happy are the people whose God is the Lord." - Psalm 144:15

MUSTARD FRIED CATFISH

Ingredients

- 3-4 catfish (whole or fillets)
- 1½ cups yellow cornmeal
- ½ cup flour
- 1 tsp each: garlic powder, onion powder, salt, pepper, and Old Bay seasoning
- 3-4 tbsp mustard
- Oil for frying (approx. 3 cups)
- Large pot

Tip

Delicious served with coleslaw and hush puppies. Place on a rack to drain or on paper towels.

MUSTARD FRIED CATFISH

Instructions

- Wash fish and pat dry.
- Coat fish with mustard on both sides.
- Season with the seasoning mixture and set aside.
- Pour oil into a large pot and heat to medium-high.
- In a separate bowl, combine cornmeal, flour, and the same seasoning mixture for dredging.
- Dredge the fish in the cornmeal mixture, making sure it is completely coated all over.
- Place fish in hot oil and fry for 3-4 minutes on each side, until golden brown, crispy, and flaky.

Enjoy!!!

QUOTE:

Only those who do nothing at all make no mistakes.

Ingredients

- 3-4 lbs beef roast or chuck roast
- 1 onion, chopped
- 1 cup baby Bella mushrooms
- 1 clove garlic, diced
- 1 tsp onion powder
- 1 tsp garlic powder
- 1 tsp Sazón seasoning
- 1 tbsp Worcestershire sauce
- ¼ cup vegetable oil
- Salt and pepper to taste
- 3 cups beef broth
- 2 tbsp cornstarch
- 2 tbsp water

BEEF TIPS AND RICE

Enjoy!!!

INSPIRATIONAL NOTE:

Flavor comes from joy. A person's true character is revealed when the pot is scratching.

BEEF TIPS AND RICE

Directions

- Preheat oven to 350°F.
- In a large skillet over medium heat, brown the roast after cutting it into small pieces.
- Season and coat beef with flour, then transfer to a large oven-safe pan, preferably a Dutch oven.
- In the same skillet, sauté the onions, mushrooms, and garlic until browned.
- Add the sautéed vegetables to the beef roast.
- Pour in the beef broth, then add Sazón seasoning, garlic powder, onion powder, Worcestershire sauce, salt, and pepper.
- Bring the mixture to a boil.
- In a small bowl, mix cornstarch and water until smooth.
- Slowly whisk the cornstarch mixture into the boiling broth mixture to thicken it.
- Pour this mixture over the roast and stir. If the roast is not covered, add more broth.
- Cover the pan with a lid and place it in the oven. Cook for 1½-2½ hours.
- Cook rice according to package instructions.
- For added flavor, cook the rice in beef broth.

NOTES

Where the Spirit of the Lord is, there is freedom.
— 2 Corinthians 3:17

BALSAMIC RASPBERRY VINAIGRETTE DRESSING

Ingredients

- 1 cup fresh raspberries
- 2 tbsp white sugar
- ¾ cup balsamic vinegar
- ¼ cup olive oil
- 2 tbsp honey
- ½ tsp salt

Instructions

- In a bowl, mix raspberries and sugar together and let sit for 10 minutes.
- Mash the berries with a fork until liquefied.
- Pour the raspberry mixture into a clean jar with a lid.
- Add balsamic vinegar, olive oil, honey, and salt.
- Secure the lid and shake until the dressing is fully mixed.
- Store in the refrigerator.

Perfect dressing for spinach salad. Enjoy!

SCRIPTURE INSPIRATIONAL:
"The joy of the Lord is your strength." - Nehemiah 8:10

Ingredients

Honey Mustard Sauce

- ½ cup yellow mustard
- 2 tbsp mayonnaise
- 3 tbsp honey
- 1 tsp dry mustard
- ½ tsp lemon juice

Instructions

HONEY MUSTARD SAUCE

- Mix all ingredients together in a bowl.
- Stir until well combined.
- For best results, chill for a couple of hours in the refrigerator before serving.
- Enjoy!

INSPIRATIONAL NOTE:
Love your family, work super hard, and live your passion.

TARTER SAUCE

Ingredients

- 1 cup mayonnaise
- 1 tbsp ground ginger
- 1 tbsp sweet pickle relish
- 1 tsp dry dill
- 2 tbsp minced onion (not dried — freshly minced)
- 1 tsp lemon juice
- 1 tsp sugar

Instructions

- Mix all ingredients well in a small bowl.
- Refrigerate for at least 10 minutes before serving.
- Tip: Excellent served over fish, shrimp, or any seafood.

INSPIRATIONAL NOTE:
Love your family, work super hard, and live your passion.

OLD FASHION POUND CAKE

Ingredients

- 2 sticks butter (softened)
- 2 cups sugar
- 1 tsp salt
- 6 eggs (room temperature)
- 2 cups all-purpose flour
- 2 tsp vanilla extract
- Bundt pan

Enjoy!!!

OLD FASHION POUND CAKE

Instructions

- Prepare the pan by spraying with baking spray or greasing and dusting with flour.
- Using a stand mixer, cream the butter and sugar together until the mixture is pale yellow and well combined.
- Add the eggs one at a time, mixing until the yolk is no longer visible before adding the next. The mixture should be light and fluffy.
- In a separate bowl, combine the salt and flour. Add to the egg mixture in three parts, beating after each addition until just combined. Be careful not to overmix.
- Add the vanilla extract and mix just until incorporated.
- Pour the batter into the prepared Bundt pan.
- Place the cake in a cold oven and set the temperature to 350°F.
- Bake for 60 minutes, or until a toothpick inserted comes out clean.
- Allow the cake to cool for 10 minutes before removing from the pan.
- Serve with your favorite fruit topping or ice cream. Either way, you won't be disappointed.

QUOTE:
If you don't stand for something, you will fall for anything.

LEMON BUTTER POUND CAKE

Ingredients

- 3 cups all-purpose flour (preferably cake flour)
- 3 cups sugar
- 1 stick butter, room temperature
- 5 eggs, room temperature
- 1 tsp vanilla extract
- 1 tsp butter extract
- 1 tbsp baking powder
- 1 tsp salt
- ⅓ cup shortening
- 1 cup whole milk
- 6 tbsp lemon juice
- 1 lemon, zested

Equipment

- Electric mixer with paddle attachment
- 1.5 cup bundt or tube pan

LEMON BUTTER POUND CAKE

Instructions

- Preheat oven to 350°F. Grease and flour a 1.5 cup bundt or tube pan.
- If using a 9 or 10 cup pan, leave ½-1 inch space at the top so the cake doesn't spill out.
- Combine dry ingredients and set aside.
- Using an electric mixer, cream together butter, shortening, and sugar. Beat until fluffy and pale yellow.
- Add eggs one at a time, beating well after each egg. No yolk should be visible.
- Add dry ingredients in 3 additions to the butter mixture, alternating with milk, beginning and ending with the flour mixture.
- Beat at low speed until blended after each addition.
- Mix in lemon juice and zest.
- Pour batter into prepared pan. Place in oven and bake until a toothpick inserted in center comes out clean, approx. 55 minutes.
- Cool cake in pan for 15 minutes, then turn out on a rack to cool completely.
- Drizzle with lemon glaze once the cake is completely cooled.

LEMON BUTTER POUND CAKE

Lemon Glaze

- ¾ cup powdered sugar
- ¼ cup lemon juice
- Zest of one lemon
- 1 tsp salted butter

Instructions

- Combine sugar, lemon juice, and lemon zest in a medium bowl. Mix until well combined.
- Add melted butter and continue to stir until lumps are gone.
- Place in microwave for 3 minutes, remove, and drizzle over the top of the cake.

ENCOURAGEMENT:

"In your time of trouble, God is your very present help. His love is your security."

FIVE FLAVOR POUND CAKE

Enjoy!!!

Ingredients

- 3 cups all-purpose flour (preferably cake flour)
- 1 cup butter
- ½ cup shortening (butter flavored)
- 3 cups sugar
- 5 large eggs (room temperature)
- 1 tsp baking powder
- ½ tsp salt
- ½ cup buttermilk
- + ½ cup half and half
- 1 tsp each of the following extracts:
  - Vanilla
  - Lemon
  - Rum
  - Coconut
  - Butter

FIVE FLAVOR POUND CAKE

Instructions

- Preheat oven to 325°F and spray a bundt pan generously with nonstick baking spray.
- Cream sugar, butter, and shortening together until light and fluffy.
- Add eggs one at a time, beating well after each addition. No yolk should be visible.
- In a separate bowl, combine dry ingredients (flour, baking powder, salt).
- Combine milk and flavorings in another bowl.
- Add ⅓ of the flour mixture to the creamed mixture and beat on medium speed.
- Add ⅓ of the milk mixture and continue beating.
- Alternate additions of flour and milk, beginning and ending with flour. Beat well after each addition.
- Pour batter into the prepared bundt pan.
- Bake in preheated oven at 325°F for 60-70 minutes or until a toothpick inserted in the center comes out clean.

FIVE FLAVOR POUND CAKE

Lemon Glaze

- 1 cup powdered sugar
- 3 tbsp half and half or whole milk
- ¼ tsp each of the five flavor extracts (vanilla, lemon, rum, coconut, butter)

Instructions

- Mix glaze ingredients in a small bowl until smooth.
- Let cake cool completely.
- Drizzle glaze over cooled cake.

Tip

Prepare bundt pan by spraying with nonstick baking spray before adding batter.

INSPIRATIONAL NOTE:

Try to get better in some way every day.

EGG PIE

Ingredients

- 3 eggs
- 1⅓ cups sugar
- 1½ tsp all-purpose flour
- 1 tsp salt
- 1 stick melted butter
- 1 tsp vanilla extract
- 1 tsp butter extract
- ½ cup whole milk
- ½ cup heavy whipping cream
- 1 (9-inch) pie crust, blind baked

Enjoy!!!

EGG PIE

Instructions

To blind bake the crust:
- Preheat oven to 400°F.
- Line the pie crust with parchment paper and fill with pie weights or dried beans.
- Bake for 10 minutes.
- Remove from oven, discard parchment and weights, and set aside to cool.
- Reduce oven temperature to 325°F.

To make the filling:
- In a medium bowl, beat eggs and set aside.
- In another bowl, combine sugar, milk, flour, salt, nutmeg (if using), vanilla extract, and butter extract.
- Beat in the eggs and stir in melted butter until fully incorporated.
- Pour the mixture into the prepared pie crust.

To bake:
- Place pie in preheated 325°F oven.
- Bake for 45-55 minutes, or until the center is set and a toothpick inserted comes out clean.
- Allow pie to cool before slicing.

KITCHEN WISDOM:
"The room for improvement is always our biggest room."

MAMA DEE'S SWEET POTATO PIE

Ingredients

- 1 stick butter
- ½ cup brown sugar
- ½ cup granulated sugar
- 1 tsp cinnamon
- 1 tsp nutmeg
- 1½ tsp vanilla extract
- 2 eggs
- 3-4 medium sweet potatoes

Tip

To prevent the edges of your crust from getting too dark, cover with foil or use a pie shield.

MAMA DEE'S SWEET POTATO PIE

Instructions

- Preheat oven to 425°F.
- Wash sweet potatoes and pat dry. Using a fork, prick holes all over each potato.
- Place potatoes on a cookie sheet and bake for
- 45 minutes.
- Remove from oven, reduce oven temperature to 350°F.
- While potatoes are still warm, peel and place in a mixing bowl. Add the butter and let it melt into the potatoes. Allow to cool slightly (about 5 minutes).
- Add the remaining ingredients and mix well with a hand mixer on high speed until the mixture is smooth.
- Pour into a blind-baked pie crust.
- Bake at 350°F for 40-45 minutes, or until the crust is golden brown and a toothpick inserted in the center comes out clean.

SCRIPTURE INSPIRATION:
"I will praise thee, O Lord, with my whole heart."
- Psalm 9:1

DEE-LICIOUS PECAN PIE

Ingredients

- Blind bake the pie crust and set it aside.
- In a mixing bowl, beat the eggs until yolk and white are combined.
- Add the sugar, corn syrup, and vanilla, stirring well to combine.
- Fold in the pecans, making sure all ingredients are mixed thoroughly.
- Pour mixture into the blind-baked pie crust.
- Reduce oven temperature to 350°F and bake for 30–35 minutes, or until the center is just barely moving when gently shaken.
- Tip: Cover the crust edges with foil or a pie shield to prevent over-browning.
- Cool before serving.
- Enjoy!

Enjoy!!!

DEE-LICIOUS PECAN PIE

Instructions

- Blind bake the pie crust and set it aside.
- In a mixing bowl, beat the eggs until yolk and white are combined.
- Add the sugar, corn syrup, and vanilla, stirring well to combine.
- Fold in the pecans, making sure all ingredients are mixed thoroughly.
- Pour mixture into the blind-baked pie crust.
- Reduce oven temperature to 350°F and bake for 30-35 minutes, or until the center is just barely moving when gently shaken.
- Tip: Cover the crust edges with foil or a pie shield to prevent over-browning.
- Cool before serving.
- Enjoy!

SCRIPTURE QUOTE:
"I will seek unto God, and unto God I commit my cause." — Job 5:8

TEA CAKES

Ingredients

- 1 cup butter
- 3 eggs, room temperature
- 3 cups all-purpose flour
- 1 tsp vanilla extract
- 2 tsp baking powder
- ¼ tsp salt

Enjoy!!!

TEA CAKES

Instructions

- Preheat oven to 375°F.
- In a large bowl, cream butter and sugar until light and fluffy. Add eggs one at a time, beating well after each addition. Add vanilla.
- In a separate bowl, combine flour, salt, and baking powder.
- Gradually add dry mixture to the creamed mixture. The dough will be soft. Cover and place in refrigerator for 2 hours to allow dough to firm up.
- Remove from refrigerator and, on a greased baking sheet, drop a ball of dough (approx. 1 tablespoon) two inches apart.
- Bake until edges are golden brown, 7-8 minutes.
- Note: Before baking, use thumb to gently press the center of ball to flatten a bit.

INSPIRATIONAL NOTES:
Sorrow looks back.
Worry looks around.
Faith looks up.

OATMEAL RAISIN COOKIES

Ingredients

- 1 cup all-purpose flour
- ½ cup butter
- ½ cup packed brown sugar
- ½ cup granulated sugar
- 1½ cups old-fashioned rolled oats
- 1 egg (room temperature)
- 1 cup raisins
- ½ tsp baking soda
- ½ tsp allspice
- ¼ tsp salt
- 1 tsp vanilla and butter extract

Enjoy!!!

OATMEAL RAISIN COOKIES

Instructions

- Preheat oven to 350°F.
- In a large bowl, whisk together flour, allspice, baking soda, and salt. Stir in the oats and set aside.
- Using a stand mixer with a paddle attachment, beat the brown sugar, granulated sugar, and butter until well combined (about 2 minutes).
- Beat in the egg and vanilla-butter extract until fluffy.
- Gradually add the flour mixture to the bowl, beating just until combined.
- Stir in the oats and raisins by hand.
- Drop 1½ teaspoons of dough on a parchment-lined baking sheet, spacing them 2 inches apart.
- Bake for 8–10 minutes or until the edges are golden brown.
- Remove from oven and let cookies cool on the baking sheet for 5 minutes, then transfer to a wire rack to cool completely.

SCRIPTURE REFLECTION:
"Do not be quickly provoked in your spirit, for anger resides in the lap of fools." — Ecclesiastes

PEANUT BUTTER CHOCOLATE CHIP COOKIES

Ingredients

- 1 ½ cups all-purpose flour
- ½ cup unsalted butter, room temperature
- ½ cup brown sugar
- 1 cup peanut butter
- ½ cup granulated sugar
- ⅔ tsp vanilla extract
- ⅛ tsp butter extract
- 1 egg
- 1 cup semi-sweet chocolate chips
- ¾ tsp baking powder

Enjoy!!!

PEANUT BUTTER CHOCOLATE CHIP COOKIES

Instructions

- Preheat oven to 350°F.
- In a small bowl, combine flour and baking powder and set aside.
- Using a stand mixer fitted with a paddle attachment, cream butter and sugars together until light and fluffy.
- Add peanut butter and mix until well incorporated.
- Mix in egg and vanilla extract.
- Add flour mixture and beat until well incorporated.
- Fold in chocolate chips using a rubber spatula.
- Roll dough into 1-inch balls and place on a parchment-lined baking sheet, two inches apart.
- Flatten slightly with a fork.
- Bake for 7-8 minutes, or until edges turn golden brown.
- Cool on cookie sheet for 5-10 minutes, then transfer to a wire rack to cool completely.

QUOTE:
You should never let adversity get you down except on your knees.

MEASURING CONVERSION TABLE

Volume	Cups	Tablespoons	Teaspoons	Milliliters
1 cup	1	16	48	240 ml
3/4 cup	0.75	12	36	180 ml
2/3 cup	0.66	10 tbsp + 2 tsp	32	160 ml
1/2 cup	0.5	8	24	120 ml
1/3 cup	0.33	5 tbsp + 1 tsp	16	80 ml
1/4 cup	0.25	4	12	60 ml
1/8 cup	0.125	2	6	30 ml
1 tablespoon (tbsp)	—	1	3	15 ml
1 teaspoon (tsp)	—	—	1	5 ml

NOTES

Where the Spirit of the Lord is, there is freedom.
— 2 Corinthians 3:17

NOTES

**Where the Spirit of the Lord is, there is freedom.
— 2 Corinthians 3:17**

NOTES

Where the Spirit of the Lord is, there is freedom.
— 2 Corinthians 3:17

www.ingramcontent.com/pod-product-compliance
Lightning Source LLC
Chambersburg PA
CBRC091205010526
44107CB00021B/1254